The Power of the 40s

Frontispiece
No. 40 084 heads the Heaton — Red Bank empty vans up the Calder Valley past Sowerby Bridge West signal box.
11th April, 1978.
G.W. Morrison

SOWERBY BRIDGE WEST

The Power of the 40s

Compiled by

J. S. Whiteley and
G. W. Morrison

Oxford Publishing Co·

Acknowledgement: The authors would like to thank all the photographers who have so kindly contributed pictures, and to the various regions of British Rail for granting facilities which made so many of these photographs possible. Particular thanks are offered to Margaret Morley for her part in typing the manuscript.

Publisher's note: This book is reprinted, as a tribute to the '40s', as originally published in 1978. The reader will appreciate that over the last 26 years there have been many changes, with seven examples surviving in preservation.

No. D249 leaves the old Leeds City station on the 9.45 am Newcastle — Liverpool express on 16th March, 1961.

G. W. Morrison

First published 1978
Reprinted 1985
This impression 2004

ISBN 0 86093 033 5

Published by Oxford Publishing Co.

an imprint of Ian Allan Publishing Ltd, Hersham, Surrey KT12 4RG.
Printed by Ian Allan Printing Ltd, Hersham, Surrey KT12 4RG.

Code: 0407/A

INTRODUCTION

To cover every aspect of the career of the 'Forties' in just over 200 pictures is no easy task, as they have worked every type of train from the 'Royal Scot', to the humble cross country pick-up, and in virtually every area of the Midland, Eastern, and Scottish regions, and indeed were still doing so in the late 1970s.

The 'Forties' must be regarded as the first successful British main line diesels, and it is for this reason we have included a little background information on the locomotives from which the 'Forties' were in many respects developed, namely 10000-10001, and 10201, 10202-10203. It cannot be said that these locomotives were prototypes of the 'Forties', but they were the forerunners, particularly as far as the mechanics were concerned, even if the looks were very different.

It is hard to believe that 20 years have passed since D200 entered service on the Great Eastern section of the Eastern region, and that no fewer than 30 years have gone since 10000 emerged from Derby works. What is even more remarkable is the fact that these fine old workhorses can still be seen in 1978, thrashing up and down the East Coast main line being driven to the limit, trying to keep out of the way of HST's and 'Deltics'.

The history of the development of the five forerunners has been well documented in other books, and it is not our intention to try and cover the ground again in this album, except to say that considering the speed with which

10000 was produced, only seven months from drawing board to delivery, the locomotive appeared to perform very well.

Fine work was also done by the Southern designed locomotives, 10201/2/3, and 10203 was developed to the point of really being a 'Forty' in most respects except in looks.

The 'Forties' started their careers under far from ideal circumstances, lack of experience on the part of crews and maintenance staff, mixed steam and diesel depots, and in many cases a fair amount of prejudice as the steam enthusiasts realised that the end was in sight for their beloved 'Pacifics'.

The East and West Coast main line expresses were virtually monopolised at various stages in the early 1960s by the 'Forties', the West Coast tending to grossly overload them, particularly in summer.

British Rail realised that before any significant improvements in journey times could be achieved on the main lines, something much more powerful was needed, and so the 'Deltics', 47's and 50's gradually took over their duties.

The 'Forties' have proved to be excellent machines, once their true capabilities and limitations were realised. As they were the first main line diesels, it is not surprising that faults had to be overcome in the first few years, but since then they have given excellent service. After the end of their booked main line duties, they have settled down to steady passenger work on the secondary routes in the original regions, but are now predominantly employed on freight, particularly in the West Riding and Lancashire areas. Twenty-five of the class were named, but these have now been removed. All were products of the famous English Electric Vulcan foundry at Newton-le-Willows, except for a batch of 20 which were built by Robert Stephenson & Hawthorns, Darlington.

I am certain that the 'Forties' will go down in history as one of the best remembered British Rail diesel classes, and it is our hope that this photographic album will give as much enjoyment to you the reader, as we have had producing it, and taking most of the photographs.

The familiar and distinctive 'whistle' of the 'Forties' was to be heard until 1985 when the last one was withdrawn. Fortunately seven have been spared the cutters torch and can be seen running on several of the county's preserved railways and also from time-to-time on the main line.

G.W. Morrison

Plate 1: Co-Co No. 10001 was completed after nationalisation in July 1948. Nos. 10000 and 10001 were rated at 1600 bhp, and weighed 127 tons 13 cwt in working order.
N. Stead Collection

Plate 2:
Southern Region 1 Co-Co 1
No. 10201, delivered in
November 1950. This locomotive
was exhibited at the 1951 Festival
of Britain. It was rated at 1750
bhp and weighed 135 tons.
OPC Collection

Plate 3: *Above* Nos. 10000 and 10001 head the up 'Royal Scot' on the northern slopes of Beattock. This photograph was probably taken in the summer of 1950 when during a period of four months, they covered 69,213 train miles, working round trips from Euston to Glasgow and back. No. 10001 received its first heavy repair in early 1951.

Dr. E.G. Ashton

Plate 4: *Below* No. 10001 at work on the Midland main line on what is probably a St. Pancras — Manchester train. It was early 1949 when the locomotive was working these trains.

N. Stead Collection

Plate 5: *Above* No. D345 on York Shed. Note the shed plate under the number at the right hand end. 11th April, 1964.   *G.W. Morrison*

Plate 6: *Left* Class 40 locomotives Nos. 40 013 and 40 042 stand inside Longsight Depot on 19th February, 1978.   *G.W. Morrison*

Plate 7: *Below* No. 40 163 and No. 40 052 line up in Crewe Works with No. 47 443 on 19th February, 1978.   *G.W. Morrison*

Plate 8: Above No. 40 118 fitted with gangway doors in the nose. One of the batch of 20 built by Robert Stephenson & Hawthorns (Darlington), photographed on 19th February, 1978.   G.W. Morrison

Plate 9: Above No. 40 130, one of the batch 40 125-40 144 fitted with the split type, four digit, nose mounted indicators and gangway doors also seen on 19th February, 1978.   G.W. Morrison

Plate 10: Below A group of 40s at Warrington, showing different nose-ends. No. 40 022 left with gangway door, No. 40 098 with filled in gangway doors and right No. 40 131 with split type indicators. 19th February, 1978.   G.W. Morrison

Plate 11: *Above* No. D346 heads the up 'Queen of Scots' Pullman as it approaches Wakefield Westgate on 24th August, 1961.   *G.W. Morrison*

WORKING THE NAMED EXPRESSES

Plate 12: *Left* No. D201 which was the first Class 40 allocated to the East Coast main line in March, 1958, and based at Hornsey depot, heads the up 'Master Cutler' Pullman near Hadley Wood in July 1959.   *D. Cross*

Plate 13: *Right* D298 working the up 'Caledonian' express, diverted via the Glasgow & South Western route passes Garrochburn Signal Box. 16th May, 1963.   *D. Cross*

Plates 14 & 15: Two shots of the down 'Royal Scot' climbing the famous West Coast main line banks. *Above* No. D383 attacks Shap past Greenholme on 12th April. 1963, and *Below* No. D382 heading towards Beattock summit at Harthope on 23rd April, 1962. Note the two different types of head board.

J.S. Whiteley

Plate 16: *Above* On a fine day No. D349 heads an up freight between Steeton and Keighley. 20th June, 1962.

G.W. Morrison

Plate 17: *Below* Winter on the Settle & Carlisle showing No. D336 passing through the cutting at Dent on a down freight, whilst No. D415 passes on an up pick-up; 15th February, 1969.

G.W. Morrison

Plate 18: *Above* No. 40 176 stands on a permanent way train, during track relaying in Elland Tunnel on the Calder Valley main line. 24th April, 1977.   *G.W. Morrison*

Plate 19: *Below* On 26th August, 1975 No. 40 154 heads a train of grain wagons past Northallerton, whilst preserved locomotive No. 6960 *Raveningham Hall* languishes in a siding with a hot box, during one of its attempts to get to Shildon for the 'Rail 150' celebrations.   *G.W. Morrison*

Plate 20: Above Despite the allocation to Gateshead of thirty Class 46 locomotives, Class 40s deputise for them very frequently, particularly in summer when not precluded by their isolated boilers, and up until 1977 the 40's have tended to dominate the Newcastle — Liverpool services. No. 40 156 of Healey Mills depot which is just ex-works, but showing slight damage to one of its side panels accelerates away from Durham with the 18.05 Newcastle — Liverpool on 12th August, 1977.   *P.J. Robinson*

THE DOWN 'ROYAL SCOT' CALLS AT CARLISLE

Plate 21: Above Left No. D373 arrives from the south, alongside a DMU from Workington.

Plate 22: Left The driver looks back for the 'right away' from the guard, whilst three enthusiasts take a close look at the locomotive.

Plate 23: Left No. D373 leaves on its way to Glasgow and passes Carlisle Number 4 box with a Class 5 waiting to work north. 13th April, 1963.
All Photographs by J.S. Whiteley

Plate 24: Above No. 40 077 passes Aberdeen South signal box
as it arrives on the 10.45 from Edinburgh on 2nd September,
1977.   *G.W. Morrison*

Plate 25: Below An immaculate Haymarket-based No. 40 165 sets
off from the 'Granite City' with the 18.13 to Edinburgh on 2nd
September, 1977.   *G.W. Morrison*

Plate 26: Above Hauling the 14.35 to Edinburgh No. 40 061 passes under the most imposing gantry of all at Ferryhill on 2nd September, 1977.   G.W. Morrison

Plate 27: Below On 21st March, 1974 No. 40 160 heads the 08.07 from Edinburgh past Ferryhill signal box.   B. Morrison

Above
No. D279, recently ex-works, pauses at Leeds (City) on the
10.02 Newcastle – Liverpool. Note how old fashioned the
driver's uniform appears compared with today's.
2nd June, 1966. *G.W. Morrison*

Above
No. 40 169 passing the site of Mirfield Shed on an up freight.
29th May, 1974. *G.W. Morrison*

Below
No. D311 passes Shap Summit at the head of an up Perth – Euston express. 24th August, 1963.

G.W. Morrison

Above
No. 40 152 passes through Princes Street Gardens,
Edinburgh on a down cement train. 7th June, 1975.
J.S. Whiteley

Below
No. 40 009 passes Dringhouses Yard, York on an up
cement train. 31st May, 1977.
G.W. Morrison

Plate 28: Above 'Light' locomotive No. 40 085 negotiates the goods-only line at Bridge Junction, Doncaster, whilst in the background the diesel depot can be seen. 22nd August, 1977.

Plate 29: Above right On 7th July, 1977 No. 40 024 approaches Doncaster on the 08.53 from Cleethorpes viewed from the top of the multi-storey car park.

Plate 30: Below right Locomotive No. 40 164 of Haymarket passes slowly between Bridge Junction and Doncaster station with a northbound freight on 8th June, 1977.

All Photographs by G.W. Morrison

Plate 31: Above The mighty Forth Bridge dwarfs No. 40 103 as it heads north with a freight. 29th May, 1976.   *B. Morrison*

Plate 32: Below An unidentified D200 crosses the river Ure, as it approaches Ripon station with a Liverpool — Newcastle express in December 1966. The line was closed about January 1967.

G.W. Morrison

Plate 33: Above An unidentified Class 40 crosses Dinting viaduct with a special on the electrified Manchester — Sheffield line. 23rd March, 1977. *G.W. Morrison*

Plate 34: Below On 6th August, 1977 No. 40 165 crosses the Royal Border Bridge at Berwick-upon-Tweed with the Saturdays only 15.10 Scarborough — Glasgow express. *G.W. Morrison*

Plate 35: Above Heading the Saturday's only 13.00 Blackpool –
Bradford No. 40 102 passes the site of Hipperholme station between
Halifax and Bradford. 2nd August, 1975.   G.W. Morrison

Plate 36: Below No. D348 banked by a 2-6-4T climbs out of Bradford
Exchange on a Grattan Warehouse special outing to Blackpool on
9th June, 1967.   G.W. Morrison

WORKING THE
HALIFAX—BRADFORD LINE

Plate 37: Right No. D396 on another Grattan Warehouse special passes Bowling Junction between Bradford and Low Moor. A class 37 is waiting to take the branch to Laisterdyke. Note the brake tender which was frequently used at this time on 40s, 37s and 20s. 9th June, 1967.   *G.W. Morrison*

Plate 38: Below On 24th July, 1976 No. 40 195 emerges from Bowling Tunnel, Bradford on the Saturdays only 13.00 Blackpool — Bradford.
                                G.W. Morrison

FORTIES WORKING UNDER THE WIRES

Plate 39: Left No. 40 020 passes Farrington Curve Junction (south of Preston) with a down parcels train. The lines to Blackburn and Ormskirk can be seen on the right. 9th April, 1977.   *G.T. Heavyside*

Plate 40: Right On 28th July, 1972 an up freight passes Winwick Junction north of Warrington hauled by No. D384. The lines on the left go to Earlestown. The signal box has now gone.   *G.T. Heavyside*

Plate 41: Left No. D232 *Empress of Canada* near Oughty Bridge on the Woodhead line, with a Manchester United football special on 14th March, 1970.
   G.W. Morrison

Plate 42: Above No. 40 182 arrives at Kings Cross under the wires which were not yet switched on. A 'Deltic' and Class 47 await their next turn of duty in the yard. 31st July, 1977.

G.W. Morrison

Plate 43: Below Passing Nunnery Junction, Sheffield on a Cleethorpes — Manchester train is No. 40 118 on 4th December, 1977.

G.W. Morrison

Plate 44: Above The Halifax Building Society's Head Office
dominates the skyline as No. 40 199 leaves Halifax Town on the
13.00 Saturdays only Blackpool — Bradford. 23rd August, 1975.
G.W. Morrison

Plate 45: Right No. 40 037 heads a down coal train for the
north west into the cutting between Newlay and Calverley
on the outskirts of Leeds, 20th May, 1977.   *G.W. Morrison*

Above
No. 40 004 races down the main line north of York at Pilmoor on a special.
28th May, 1977.
J.S. Whiteley

Above
No. 40 171 passes Holgate Road Bridge, York on a returning excursion to Lancashire. 26th May, 1977.
G.W. Morrison

Below
No. D384 crosses Ribblehead viaduct at the head of a Birmingham — Glasgow express which had to be diverted off the West Coast main line. 4th April, 1965.
G.W. Morrison

Above
No. 40 051 on a heavy freight approaches Normanton. 8 June, 1977.

G.W. Morrison

Right
Wintry weather on the Settle – Carlisle as No. D268 passes Blea Moor on an up freight. 14th February, 1970.

G.W. Morrison

Below
No. 40 025 passes through the old marshalling yard between Whitehall Junction and Farnley, Leeds on an up parcels train. 25th July, 1976.

G.W. Morrison

IN THE WESTMORLAND FELLS

Plate 46: *Above* No. D255 overflows on the troughs at Dillicar as it speeds south on the 09.00 Perth — Euston. 12th April, 1963.   *J.S. Whiteley*

Plate 47: *Left* Viewed from inside Thrimby Grange signal box a D200 climbs to Shap Summit with the 09.00 Perth — Euston. 30th March, 1964.   *J.S. Whiteley*

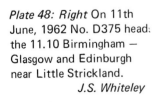

Plate 48: *Right* On 11th June, 1962 No. D375 heads the 11.10 Birmingham — Glasgow and Edinburgh near Little Strickland.
J.S. Whiteley

Plate 49: Above On what is normally a Class 47 duty No. 40 077 is seen near Aycliffe on the East Coast main line heading a rake of air braked coal empties to Widdrington. 18th November, 1977.

P.J. Robinson

Plate 50: Left No. D369 passes Dalrymple Junction, 3 miles south of Ayr on the Stranraer line. It is at the top of a 1 in 70 climb, with a train of new cars. 2nd July, 1966.   D. Cross

Plate 51: Above Passing the site of Horbury and Ossett station (closed on 5th January, 1970) No. 40 007 heads a ballast train from the east into Healey Mills yard. 18th May, 1977.

J.S. Whiteley

Plate 52: Below No. 40 196 passes through the deep cutting at Horbury towards the east, with some empty coal wagons. 22nd April, 1977.

G.W. Morrison

Plate 53: Above On 22nd April, 1977 No. 40 148 trundles towards Wakefield Kirkgate away from the yard which can be seen in the background.

G.W. Morrison

Plate 54: Below A few days later No. 40 124 approaches the yard with some unfitted coal wagons from a local mine, without a brake van. 27th April, 1977.

G.W. Morrison

ARRIVALS AND DEPARTURES AT HEALEY MILLS MARSHALLING YARD

Plate 55: Above A Tyne yard to Carlisle freight-hauled by No. 40 073
runs alongside the banks of the Tyne river near Blaydon in 1977.

P.J. Robinson

Plate 56: Left There seems to be something wron
with No. 40 034 as it struggles away from
Newcastle after a lengthy stop with the 09.50
Dundee — Kings Cross relief. It is seen here
negotiating King Edward Bridge Junction on
3rd January, 1977. *P.J. Robinson*

DOUBLE HEADING

Plate 57: Above On 14th July, 1962 No. D292 is piloting Class 5 4-6-0 No. 45173 between Crawford and Elvanfoot, heading an up Glasgow — Manchester express.

G.W. Morrison

Plate 58: Above No. D390 piloting Class 25 No. D5170 climb out of Leeds past Whitehall Junction on the 07.50 Kings Cross to Bradford on 29th September, 1967. *G.W. Morrison*

Plate 59: Below No. 40 124 pilots No. 40 159 on a down express near Thirsk, 13th June, 1977. *B. Morrison*

Plate 60: Above On a glorious summer's day No. 40 142 heads an up freight near Lamberton Beach. 3rd June, 1976. *L.A. Nixon*

Plate 61: Below No. 40 162 passes on a down tanker train at the same location also photographed on 3rd June, 1976. *L.A. Nixon*

Plate 62: Above No. 40 050 skims along the clifftops with the lightweight 15.00 (SO) Edinburgh — Newcastle. 31st July, 1976.

P.J. Robinson

Plate 63: Below Heavier work for No. 40 153 as it heads north on a Scarborough — Glasgow relief. 31st July, 1976. *P.J. Robinson*

CLIMBING THE BANKS

Plate 64: Beattock. On 14th July, 1962 No. D384 passes the summit with an up Glasgow — Manchester express.
G.W. Morrison

Plate 65: Blea Moor. Heading the diverted down 'Royal Scot' on the last few yards to the summit is No. D336 seen on 4th April 1965.

G.W. Morrison

Plate 66: Ais Gill. No. D330 passes the summit board on the diverted 'Royal Scot' on 4th April, 1965. *G.W. Morrison*

Plate 67: Grayrigg. On 6th August, 1966 No. D335 hurries down the hill past the loop at Grayrigg on the up 09.00 Perth — Euston.

G.W. Morrison

Plate 68: Shap. A Euston — Carlisle express hauled by No. D291 emerges from the cutting at the summit on 24th August, 1963.

G.W. Morrison

Plate 69: Above The woollen mills and general panorama of Brighouse overshadow No. 40 176 as it trundles back to Healey Mills yard after working through the night and day on a permanent way train which was relaying track in Elland Tunnel. 24th April, 1977.
G.W. Morrison

Plate 70: Below No. 40 147 threads its way eastwards down the S-bend at Thornhill Junction, on the ex-Lancashire and Yorkshire line, with a train of new Ford cars on 23rd July, 1976.
G.W. Morrison

WEST RIDING FREIGHT

Plate 71: *Above* On 18th May, 1977 No. 40 176 approaches Goose Hill Junction, Normanton off the ex-Lancashire and Yorkshire main line, whilst a train of coal empties heads south down the Midland main line headed by a Class 37.
G.W. Morrison

Plate 72: *Below* Approaching Thackley Tunnel near Shipley No. 40 100 heads an up ballast train from the Swindon quarry on the old Grassington branch. 20th May, 1977.
G.W. Morrison

Plate 73: Left No. 40 049
leaves Leeds on the 10.02
Newcastle — Liverpool, whilst
No. 40 016 runs round a
recently arrived parcels train
from the north, and No. 45 026
waits to take over the 10.20
Nottingham — Glasgow. 8th
February, 1977.
G.W. Morrison

Plate 74: Below No. 40 197
leaves Sowerby Bridge with
the 13.00 Saturdays only
Blackpool — Bradford on 21st
August, 1976. *G.W. Morrison*

Plate 75: *Above* The 'Granite City' overshadows No. 40 184 as it pulls out on the 17.35 Aberdeen — Glasgow (Queen Street) express. 2nd September, 1977.   *G.W. Morrison*

Plate 76: *Below* No. 40 162 ambles away from Newcastle over Byker Bridge with the 11.10 Saturdays only Newcastle to Edinburgh. 7th August, 1976.   *P.J. Robinson*

Plate 77: *Above* Inside Haymarket depot No. 40 158 awaits attention alongside Class 24 No. 24 118. 19th April, 1976.
G.W. Morrison

Plate 79: *Above right* On 20th April, 1976 No. 40 060 heads an up Aberdeen — Edinburgh express as it approaches Dalmeny Junction, with the Forth Bridge showing in the background.
G.W. Morrison

Plate 78: *Below* Class 40's Nos. 40 165, 40 101, and 40 017 dominate the scene at Ferryhill depot, Aberdeen together with a Class 26 and Class 47. 3rd September, 1977.
G.W. Morrison

Plate 80: *Below right* Leaving Arbroath and heading north No. 40 162 leads a down parcels train for Aberdeen. 3rd September, 1977.
G.W. Morrison

THE EAST COAST MAIN LINE

Plates 81 & 82: Two photographs showing No. D273 and No. D256 working up and down expresses on the East Coast main line past now demolished stations. *Right* Grantshouse and *Below* Reston between Berwick and Edinburgh. 13th July, 1961.   *G.W. Morrison*

Plates 83 & 84: Up and down expresses passing through the Lune Gorge on 18th August, 1962. *Above* No. D336 heads the up 09.00 Perth — Euston round the curve at Low Gill, whilst *Below* No. D214 *Antonia* accelerates down Dillicar Straight towards Tebay before tackling Shap bank.

G.W. Morrison

Plate 85: Above Hauling the 09.42 Saturdays Only Newcastle — Manchester No. 40 046 climbs out of Huddersfield towards Marsden through Paddock Cutting, on 4th June, 1977.

G.W. Morrison

Plate 86: Below No. 40 003 emerges from Standedge Tunnel on a summer Saturdays Only Manchester — Newcastle, 23rd August, 1975.

G.W. Morrison

TRANS-
PENNINE
EXPRESSES

Plate 87: Above On 18th May, 1977 No. 40 024 passes Batley on the 08.10 Liverpool – Newcastle. The familiar West Riding terrace houses show clearly in the background.
G.W. Morrison

Plate 88: Right Haymarket Class 40 No. 40 161 provides unusual power for the 15.10 Liverpool — Newcastle as it approaches Mirfield, having just passed underneath the ex-Lancashire-Yorkshire Calder Valley main line. In the background can be seen the remains of the viaduct that used to carry the 'new' LNW line to Leeds. 18th August, 1976. *G.W. Morrison*

Plate 89: The empty coaching stock of the 08.10 Liverpool hauled by No. 40 151 heads for Heaton carriage sidings as it leaves Newcastle on 14th May, 1977.

J.S. Whiteley

Plate 90: No. 40 009 approaches Newcastle from the north with an up express. Note the elevated speed restriction signs on the gantry. 16th July, 1977.   *L.A. Nixon*

Plate 91: Above On 17th July, 1976 No. 40 159 rushes through
Berwick-upon-Tweed with the 15.10 (SO) summer Scarborough
— Glasgow. This was up until 1977 a regular Class 40 working,
the out and back journey in the day covering about 560 miles.

P.J. Robinson

Plate 92: Below No. 40 068 negotiates the curves between
Burnmouth and Grantshouse with a down special on 17th August,
1977.

J.S. Whiteley

Plate 93: Above On a frosty December morning No. 40 164 approaches Newcastle over Byker Bridge with the 08.00 Edinburgh — Newcastle stopping train. Note the Royal Mail vehicles at the front of the train. 11th December, 1976.   *P.J. Robinson*

Plate 94: Below No. 40 165 at speed near Belford on the 07.39 (SO) Glasgow (Queen Street) — Scarborough on 6th August, 1977.
C.J. Morrison

Plate 95: *Above* An up Glasgow — Euston sleeper pauses at
Carlisle during the night; No. D372 is at the head on 29th
March, 1964.   *J.S. Whiteley*

Plate 96: *Below* No. 40 042 is receiving attention inside Longsight
Depot on 19th February, 1978.   *G.W. Morrison*

Plate 97: *Above* On 18th August, 1962 No. D243 pulls out of the now closed Manchester (Exchange), with the early morning Newcastle — Liverpool train. Patricroft Standard Class 5's await their next duties in the background.   *J.S. Whiteley*

Plate 98: *Below* No. 40 115 arrives at Manchester (Victoria) on a dismal damp day, with the 12.50 from Blackpool. 19th July, 1976.
G.T. Heavyside

Plate 99: *Above* On 3rd May, 1969 No. D348 pauses at Welshpool on a Railway Correspondence and Travel Society special from Leeds to the Tallylyn railway. *G.W. Morrison*

Plate 100: *Below* No. 40 179 hauls one of the Settle & Carlisle centenary specials, with preserved coaches from Steamtown, Carnforth past Horton-in-Ribblesdale. 1st May, 1976. *G.W. Morrison*

Plate 101: *Above* Taking the through road at Bangor station No. D376 makes an impressive sight with a down Manchester — Holyhead boat train in July 1966.   *B. Wynne*

Plate 102: *Below* A shabby looking No. D305 leaves the Menai Bridge with an up relief to the 'Irish Mail' in September, 1969.   *B. Wynne*

FORERUNNERS IN ACTION!

Plate 103: Left No. 10000 heads a Euston — Bletchley stopping train which at this date were regularly hauled by the various forerunners based at Willesden. June 1960.
D. Cross

Plate 104: Left The most powerful of the forerunners, 2000 hp No. 10203 heads a Euston — Rugby semi-fast train near Kenton in June 1960.
D. Cross

Plate 105: Left No. 10201 passes Kilburn High Road on a down Euston — Bletchley local, August 1960.
D. Cross

Plate 106: Above Nos. 10001 and 10000 pass Lichfield on the down 'Royal Scot'. It was about this time that these two locomotives finished their regular working in multiple on the Scottish expresses, the last occasion being in March 1958. 20th July, 1957.   D.J. Montgomery Collection

Plate 107: Below Nos. 10201 and 10202 head south from Rugby on what is probably the up 'Royal Scot'. These locomotives only worked double-headed on very few occasions. June 1957.
                                    D.J. Montgomery Collection

Plate 108: Above An unusual view of Edinburgh (Waverley) with No. 40 050 waiting to depart on the 14.45 to Aberdeen on 1st June, 1977.

B. Morrison

Plate 109: *Right* No. 40 146 waits patiently in Glasgow (Central) at the head of an up express to Leeds. 25th June, 1974. *D. Cross*

Plate 110: *Left* Class 40 No. D334 pulls out of Stirling on the up 09.00 Perth — London Euston express. 20th April, 1965.
J.S. Whiteley

Plate 111: *Below* On 14th August, 1965 No. D359 pauses at Perth with an up express from Dundee to Glasgow (Queen Street). *G.W. Morrison*

Plate 112: *Above* No. D294 approaches Llandudno Junction with a Euston — Holyhead express, whilst in the background a dmu from Betws-y-Coed waits to join the main line. 22nd June, 1963.
G.W. Morrison

Plate 113: *Below* Heading for North Wales No. 40 182 crosses the River Dee leaving Chester with a summer Saturdays Only train. 27th August, 1977.
L.A. Nixon

Plate 114: Right No. D379 leaves Chester General round the south side of the triangle on the 08.30 Euston — Llandudno on 30th May, 1964.
J.S. Whiteley

Plate 115: Left The up 'Irish Mail' passes Saltney Junction on the outskirts of Chester behind No. D291 on 7th August, 1961. *J.S. Whiteley*

Plate 116: Right No. D223 *Lancastria* leaves Llandudno Junction with an up express on 9th August, 1960.
D. Cross

Plate 117: Left The 10.40 (SO) Manchester — Newcastle hauled by No. 40 183 passes Chaloners Whin Junction south of York on 3rd September, 1977.

J.S. Whiteley

Plate 118: Right No. D351 arrives at platform 9, York from the north with the up 'Northumbrian' on 28th April, 1962.   *J.S. Whiteley*

Plate 119: Left On 16th June, 1962 No. D352 heads south through York with an up express freight. In the background can be seen the old steam roundhouse.   *G.W. Morrison*

Plate 120: Above No. 40 015 rounds the curve at Clifton north of York on the 10.10 Liverpool — Newcastle. The Minster can be seen in the background. 11th December, 1976.   J.S. Whiteley

Plate 121: Below No. 40 176 passes Dringhouses yard south of the station with an up freight on 26th May, 1977.   J.S. Whiteley

Plate 122: Above Heading for Scarborough No. 40 084 rounds
the curve at Kirkham Abbey with a summer Saturdays Only
express. 17th July, 1976.   *G.W. Morrison*

Plate 123: Below No. 40 159 negotiates the bend at Kirkham
Abbey on the banks of the river Derwent as it heads west with a
relief to the 15.10 Saturdays Only Scarborough — Glasgow. 17th
July, 1976.   *G.W. Morrison*

Plate 124: Right Deep in the woods alongside the banks of
the river Derwent No. 40 155 takes it very slowly round the
sharp curves near Castle Howard at the head of the Saturdays
Only 07.39 Glasgow (Queen Street) — Scarborough. 17th
July, 1976.   *G.W. Morrison*

Plate 125: *Above* An impressive view of No. 40 149 as it threads its way out of Kings Cross on the 08.30 departure for Grimsby and Cleethorpes. 12th June, 1975.   *B. Morrison*

Plate 126: *Below* No. D243 at the peak of its career passes Hadley Wood on the down 'Talisman' 16.00 Kings Cross — Edinburgh in September 1960.   *D. Cross*

Plate 127: Above In the days before the yellow end panels No. D257 races through Ganwick on a down London — Newcastle express. 13th June, 1961.   *D. Cross*

Plate 128: Below No. 40 074 takes a rest at Peterborough in the yard just north of the station, with the cathedral dominating the skyline. 16th October, 1976.   *G.W. Morrison*

THE NAMED FORTIES IN ACTION

Plate 129: No. D231 *Sylvania* accelerates a Euston — Perth express away from Oxenholme and starts to climb Grayrigg bank on 30th July, 1965. *D. Cross*

Plate 130: Left Nameplate of No. D233.
  A.C. Baker

Plate 131: Below No. D233 *Empress of England* tackles the last few hundred yards of the climb to Ais Gill summit on a diverted Glasgow — Birmingham express on 4th April, 1965. *G.W. Morrison*

Plate 132: *Above* Passing New Cummock on the Glasgow and South Western main line No. D215 *Aquitania* heads a football special from London on 11th April, 1963. *D. Cross*

Plate 133: *Below* No. D220 *Franconia* heads a 16 coach Glasgow — Leeds football special past Rodley & Calverley. Had No. D220 taken this heavy load over the Settle & Carlisle unassisted? Unfortunately we have not got the answer. 1st April, 1970. *G.W. Morrison*

Plate 134: Left No. 10000 in the black livery having lost the LMS letters and before receiving the BR lion emblem, heads an up Bletchley — Euston local past Kenton in June 1960.   *D. Cross*

Plate 135: Right Sporting the BR green livery No. D267 passes Tebay on an up Carlisle — Euston express. The steam shed can be seen clearly in the background. 5th August, 1961.   *D. Cross*

Plate 136: Below In the standard British Rail blue livery No. 40 069 emerges from the east end of Standedge Tunnel on the 18.00 Sundays Only Manchester — Newcastle. One of the two disused single bore tunnels can be seen on the left, and the canal which emerges from under the main tunnel just to the right of the signal. 20th July, 1975.
G. W. Morrison

Plate 137: *Above* The southern ascent, which is much steeper than the northern approach. The 1 in 75 is being tackled by No. D325 heading the down 'Royal Scot'.

J.S. Whiteley

Plate 138: *Right* No. D220 *Franconia* approaches from the north through the lovely scenery of the upper Clyde Valley, and is seen here near Crawford on a Glasgow — Birmingham express on 15th April, 1963. *J.S. Whiteley*

Plate 139: *Left* The climbing is over for No. D323, as it races down the bank over Harthope viaduct on the up 'Mid-day Scot'. 15th April, 1963. *J.S. Whiteley*

THE INDUSTRIAL WEST RIDING OF YORKSHIRE

Plate 140: Above A recently ex-works No. 40 152 climbs the bank to the summit in Morley Tunnel, between Dewsbury and Batley on the 10.10 Liverpool — Newcastle. 8th July, 1976.
G.W. Morrison

Plate 141: Left On 25th July, 1976 No. 40 050 passes Bradley Junction near Huddersfield on the Sundays Only 18.00 Manchester — Newcastle. The single line in the foreground forms the triangle onto the Calder Valley main line.
G.W. Morrison

Plate 142: Above Right No. 40 148 drifts down the bank from Marsden to Huddersfield near Longwood on the Sundays Only 18.00 Manchester — Newcastle. 17th June, 1976.
G.W. Morrison

Plate 143: Below Right No. 40 025 approaches Paddock on the outskirts of Huddersfield on the Saturdays Only 09.00 Llandudno — York. Longwood viaduct can be seen in the background. 16th July, 1977. *G.W. Morrison*

Plate 144: Above Ex-works Healey Mills No. 40 156 stands in the yard at Holbeck Depot, Leeds on 13th September, 1977.

G.W. Morrison

Plate 145: Below On 3rd March, 1970 No. D270 arrives at Leeds (Central) with the Harrogate portion of an up express to Kings Cross, whilst passengers in the Bradford section wait for the coaches to be attached. Note the interesting signal gantry.

G.W. Morrison

Plate 146: *Above* The changing railway and surrounding scene is well illustrated in these two pictures taken 14 years apart. No. D253 is seen on a crew training special approaching Wortley Junction, Leeds. This train used to go to Appleby and back every week day. 14th March, 1963.   *G.W. Morrison*

Plate 147: *Below* All that remains of the track layout in 1977 at the same location, showing a DMU from Harrogate travelling alongside No. 40 087 on an up parcels train from Bradford (Forster Square). 17th September, 1977.   *J.S. Whiteley*

IN AND AROUND LEEDS

Plate 148: Above On 25th June, 1966 No. D265 heads an Army Vehicle Special near Fountain Hall on the now closed 'Waverley' route.   D. Cross

Plate 149: Above No. 40 151 leaves Ipswich at the head of a light air-braked freight from Parkeston to Whitemoor. 14th October, 1977.   G.T. Heavyside

Plate 150: Above Approaching Preston from the north No. D344 heads a Blackpool — Manchester parcels. 23rd May, 1968.   D. Cross

Plate 151: Above No. D369 passes Shap Summit on a train of new lorries built in Scotland, and no doubt heading for the Midlands to be completed. 27th June, 1964.
J.S. Whiteley

Plate 152: Left Still in green livery, 12-13 years after the introduction of the British Rail standard blue, No. 40 136 trundles through Wigan Wallgate at the head of a down coal train on 23rd September, 1976. This was the penultimate Class 40 to retain this livery. No. 40 106 was still in green at the start of 1978.
B. Morrison

Plate 154: Left No. 40 100 proceeds up the East Coast main line on a freight passing Darlington station. 14th May, 1977.   *J.S. Whiteley*

Plate 155: Below No. D282 heads an express down freight for the north near the top of Stoke Bank between Peterborough and Grantham on 21st July, 1962.   *G.W. Morrison*

Plate 156: Above On 28th May, 1977 No. 40 167 heads a down parcels near Gleneagles. *B. Morrison*

Plate 157: Below No. 40 161 leaves Carrbridge on the 12.10 Inverness — Edinburgh and overtakes No. 40 001 waiting in the station on an up freight. 31st May, 1977. *B. Morrison*

Plate 158: Above In the evening light No. D296 pulls away from Gleneagles on a Euston — Perth express. 11th May, 1963.
G.W. Morrison

Plate 159: Below No. D320 climbs the 1 in 79 out of Glasgow (Buchanan Street) past St Rollox motive power depot on a down Aberdeen express. 27th March, 1964.
G.W. Morrison

**AROUND
SCOTLAND**

Plate 160: Below A meeting on the Glasgow and South Western main line at Closeburn between No 283 on a Newcastle — Stranraer train and Class 50 No. D441 on a Glasgow — Liverpool train. 17th July, 1961.
D. Cross

Plate 161: *Above* No. 40 161 of Haymarket heads southwards past Riccall near Selby. 18th August, 1976.   *G.W. Morrison*

FREIGHT ON THE EAST COAST MAIN LINE

Plate 162: *Below* On 8th June, 1977 No. 40 125 pauses in the loop at Selby Canal Junction to let the up 'Silver Jubilee' overtake.   *G.W. Morrison*

Plate 163: *Above* No. D283 at the head of a short freight heads south on the slow line near Benningborough just north of York. 6th August, 1961.   *G.W. Morrison*

Plate 164: *Below* No. 40 085 passes through Doncaster with an empty grain train from the Scottish Highlands to East Anglia. The 'Plant' can be seen in the background. 22nd June, 1977.
                          G.W. Morrison

AROUND SHEFFIELD

Plate 165: Above No. 40 198 takes the slow line past Kiveton Park station on a very light van train in July 1976. This is on the old Great Central main line.   *L.A. Nixon*

Plate 166: Left Heading a train of empty wagons for the cement works at Hope, No. 40 155 passes Blackburn Meadows near Rotherham. 2nd June, 1977.

G.W. Morrison

Plate 167: Above No. 40 193 passes Rotherham Road signal box on a mixed freight for the north. Two Class 20's can be seen in the background waiting to leave the loop. 2nd June, 1977.
G.W. Morrison

Plate 168: Below A morning Cleethorpes — Manchester train hauled by No. 40 012 approaches Rotherham past Masboro' Station North Junction signal box on 15th September, 1977.
G.W. Morrison

Plate 169: Above No. 40 092 heads west out of Chester past No. 6 signal box with a summer Saturdays Only express from the West Riding of Yorkshire. 27th August, 1977.   *L.A. Nixon*

Plate 170: Below No. 40 199 has just passed Chester Race course and heads for the North Wales coast on 27th August, 1977.   *L.A. Nixon*

THE NORTH WALES
COAST OUT OF CHESTER

Plate 171: Right On 27th August, 1977 No. 40 052 crosses the canal on the western outskirts of Chester en route to the coast.   *L.A. Nixon*

Plate 172: Below Chester No. 6 box viewed from the other side from plate 169, showing No. 40 092 accelerating away westwards. The lines from Birkenhead can be seen trailing in on the left. 27th August, 1977.
                                                    L.A. Nixon

Plates 173 & 174: No. 40 057 arrives from the north, and below is seen leaving on the Lincoln line whilst Class 47 No. 47 412 overtakes on the 12.30 Leeds — Kings Cross. 2nd February, 1977.
G.W. Morrison

BLACK CARR JUNCTION

Plate 175: Above No. 40 146 crosses Chester-le-Street viaduct on an up permanent way train on 28th September, 1975.
G.W. Morrison

Plate 176: Above Another view of No. 40 146 on the same p.w. train crossing Plawsworth viaduct, 28th September, 1975. L.A. Nixon

Plate 177: Below No. D365 crossing Montrose viaduct on an up Aberdeen — Edinburgh express on 5th August, 1972.
D. Cross

Two views showing the complex layouts at the west and east ends of Edinburgh (Waverley) before the alterations were carried out about 1976.

Plate 178: Above No. D250 leaves with the 17.25 to Dundee on 22nd July, 1963.   *J.S. Whiteley*

Plate 179: Below An unidentified D200 departs on the 10.20 to Newcastle on 22nd July, 1963.   *J.S. Whiteley*

Plate 180: Right No. 40 152 heads north through Princes Street Gardens on a cement train, 7th June, 1975.

G.W. Morrison

Plate 181: Below Still in the green livery No. 40 052 passes through the Gardens as it arrives from the north on 24th May, 1975.

G.W. Morrison

Plate 182: Above On 8th May, 1977 No. 40 095 passes Drig just north of Ravenglass on a northbound freight of hoppers.

G.W. Morrison

Plate 183: Below No. 40 017 heads past Arnside on a similar train to that in plate 182. 22nd May, 1976.

B. Morrison

FREIGHT ON THE CUMBRIAN COAST

Plate 184: Right No. 40 003 arrives under the wires at Carlisle Kingmoor yard with a freight from the north-east in October 1974. *P.J. Robinson*

Plate 185: Below No. 40 017 again seen on a train of hoppers on a dull and misty day as it heads north near Silecroft on 22nd May, 1976.
L.A. Nixon

Plate 186: *Left* An unidentified Class 40 races past Alne on the 08.10 Liverpool — Newcastle on 11th April, 1977. *J.S. Whiteley*

Plate 187: *Right* Haymarket Class 40 No. 40 184 nearly showing its number in the indicator panel approaches Sessay on a north bound parcels on 12th October, 1977. *G.W. Morrison*

Plate 188: *Below* No. 40 156 coasts round the curve at Clifton, York with the up Heaton — Red Bank parcels, 26th September, 1976. *J.S. Whiteley*

EAST COAST MAIN LINE BETWEEN NEWCASTLE AND YORK

Plate 189: Right No. 40 049 overtakes Class 37 No. 37 078 as it passes Bensham on the Saturdays Only 08.35 Newcastle — Yarmouth, 6th August, 1977. *G.W. Morrison*

Plate 190: Below On 26th March, 1978 No. 40 168 passes Heworth on the Heaton — Red Bank parcels. *P.J. Robinson*

Plate 191: Above left No. 40 194 on a southbound freight passes Class 46 No. 46 050 going north at Masboro' South Junction, Rotherham. 9th November, 1976.   *L.A. Nixon*

Plate 192: Below left In this view No. 40 194 is seen as it passes under the impressive signal gantry at Masboro' South Junction, Rotherham. 9th November, 1976.   *L.A. Nixon*

Plate 193: Right No. 40 092 passes Masboro' Station North Junction box as it heads south on a train of empty wagons on 15th September, 1977.
                              G.W. Morrison

FREIGHT AROUND SHEFFIELD AND ROTHERHAM

Plate 194: Below Ex-works No. 40 040 just past Attercliffe Road station, Sheffield and about to pass under the ex-Great Central main line, heads for the cement works in the Hope Valley. 27th May, 1977.   *L.A. Nixon*

Plate 195: Left No. D218 *Carmania,*
here seen without nameplate, passes
Kenton on a London Euston —
Manchester express in June 1960.
D. Cross

Plate 196: Right Deep in the woods
near Thrimby Grange No. D377 hauls a
heavy 09.00 Perth — Euston express
towards Shap Summit. 11th June, 1962.
J.S. Whiteley

Plate 197: Left No. D319 arrives at
Carlisle from the north with the up
'Mid-day Scot'. 13th April, 1963.
J.S. Whiteley

Plate 198: Right On 26th July, 1963 No. D216 *Campania* at Peat Lane on a Crewe — Carlisle parcels. *D. Cross*

Plate 199: Left No. 10201 leaves Basford Hall sidings, Crewe with a southbound freight on 29th April, 1961. *J.S. Whiteley*

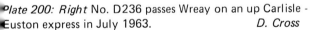

Plate 200: Right No. D236 passes Wreay on an up Carlisle - Euston express in July 1963. *D. Cross*

Plate 201: Left Here No. D236 heads an up Manchester — Euston express just south of Watford Gap on the M1 which is looking very empty by today's standards. 8th June, 1960. *D. Cross*

MAIN LINES
BETWEEN LANCASHIRE
AND YORKSHIRE

Plate 202: Left Passing Torside on the Woodhead route No. D232 *Empress of Canada* heads a Manchester United football special for Sheffield, 14th March, 1970
G.W. Morrison

Plate 203: Below No. 40 075 heads the Heaton — Red Bank empty newspaper train up the Calder Valley past Elland on 12th April, 1978.
G.W. Morrison

Plate 204: Right On 10th December, 1977 No. 40 112 arrives at Earles Sidings in the Hope Valley with an empty cement train from the west.   *L.A. Nixon*

Plate 205: Below The smoking terraced houses of Mossley dominate the scene as No. 40 025 winds its way towards Standedge on a Coventry – York football special on 26th February, 1977.

L.A. Nixon

DEPARTING FROM LEEDS

Plate 206: Left In the early livery carried by these engines No. D236 emerges from Marsh Lane Cutting near Neville Hill, Leeds on the morning Liverpool – Newcastle train. This train would have been routed via Wetherby and Harrogate. 10th March, 1961.
G.W. Morrison

Plate 207: Below left Deep in Marsh Lane Cutting No. 40 049 accelerates the 08.50 Liverpool – Newcastle away from Leeds. 26th June, 1977.
G.W. Morrison

Plate 208: Right A very clean green liveried No. D279 waits for the 'right away' from Leeds (City) on the 10.02 Newcastle – Liverpool, 2nd June, 1966.
G.W. Morrison

Plate 209: Below No. D257 passes over the LNW Dewsbury line as it climbs towards the summit at Birstall on the 'new line' to Huddersfield with the 10.02 Newcastle – Liverpool. The M621 is now built over this spot. Farnley Junction steam depot can be seen in the background on the left. 20th July, 1962.
G.W. Morrison

Plate 210: Above No. 40 144 just ex-works passes through the yard at Clifton, York with a grain train bound for Scotland, while No. 40 046 heads in the opposite direction with an up freight. 5th April, 1978.   *G.W. Morrison*

FREIGHT THROUGH CLIFTON YARD, YORK

Plate 211: Right No. 40 092 backs a train into the permanent way department sidings at Clifton on 10th October, 1976. *G.W. Morrison*

Plate 212: Below On 5th April, 1978 recently ex-works No. 40 155 passes non-stop through the north end of Clifton yard with a train of cement wagons.   *G.W. Morrison*

Plate 213: Left No. D300 leaves Marsh Lane Cutting, Leeds as it heads north with a morning Liverpool — Newcastle express. 1st May, 1962. *G.W. Morrison*

Plate 214: Right No. D284 leaves Doncaster with a Lowestoft — York express; a DMU for Hull waits in the bay on 14th May, 1963. *J.S. Whiteley*

Plate 215: Left The up 'Queen of Scot Pullman hauled by No. D359 passes th now demolished station at Beeston near Leeds on 6th June, 1962.

G.W. Morrison

Plate 216: Right No. D244 approaches Ripon station past the signal box with the 09.45 Newcastle — Liverpool express on 3rd April, 1965. The line was closed about January 1967 and these trains diverted down the East Coast main line to York.   *G.W. Morrison*

Plate 217: Below On 11th April, 1961 No. D278 climbs the bank into Harrogate with the 09.45 Newcastle express, while an 08 shunter marshalls coal wagons.   *G.W. Morrison*

Plate 218: Below An impressive view of the Calder Valley showing No. 40 030 heading a Daisy Hill — Scarborough special past Charlestown near Hebden Bridge on 15th April, 1978.

G.W. Morrison

Plate 219: *Right* No. 40 075 heads the Heaton — Red Bank empty van train under the M62 motorway where it crosses the Calder Valley near Brighouse. The track-bed of the two lines lifted can be seen clearly. 15th April, 1978. *G.W. Morrison*

Plate 220: *Below* Another view of No. 40 075 again on the Red Bank empty van train as it enters Sowerby Bridge station. Clearly standing out on the skyline is Wainhouse Tower at King Cross, Halifax. It was built in the 1800s by a wealthy businessman who wished to look into his neighbour's garden after he had built a high wall to prevent him! 12th April, 1978.   *G.W. Morrison*

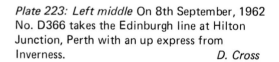

Plate 221: Above left No. 40 017 awaits the next duty at Aberdeen Ferryhill depot, 3rd September, 1977.   *G.W. Morrison*

Plate 222: Above right No. 40 061 rests in the yard at Arbroath after failing on an Edinburgh — Aberdeen express on 3rd September, 1977.   *G.W. Morrison*

Plate 223: Left middle On 8th September, 1962 No. D366 takes the Edinburgh line at Hilton Junction, Perth with an up express from Inverness.   *D. Cross*

Plate 224: Below left A very clean No. 40 063 of Haymarket enters Newtonmore in the Highlands with the 12.15 Inverness — Glasgow (Queen Street) express. 28th May, 1976.   *B. Morrison*

Plate 225: Right An unusual view of No. 40 195 as it passes the site of Horbury and Ossett station as it makes its approach to Healey Mills marshalling yard on a light freight, 30th September, 1977. *L.A. Nixon*

Plate 226: Below left: No. 40 176 passes under the wires at Elsecar Junction, Wath on a freight whilst a Class 37 waits to join the main line. 7th September, 1977.
J.S. Whiteley

Plate 227: Below right: Light work for No. 254 as it passes Dyce Junction north of Aberdeen on the 11.10 Aberdeen — Inverurie freight. 22nd November, 1972.
B. Morrison

Plate 228: Above On 4th April, 1978 No. 40 169 heads a down freight towards Healey Mills past the site of the marshalling yard at Mirfield.   *G.W. Morrison*

Plate 229: Below No. 40 196 hauls a rake of empty coal wagons from the power station back to the colliery at Walton junction, Wakefield. In the background the old steam depot can clearly be seen and for a time was used for wagon repairs. 21st March 1978.   *G.W. Morrison*

Plate 230: Above No. 40 154 comes to the aid of Class 46 No. 46 055 which had failed climbing the 1 in 105 bank from Huddersfield to Marsden on the 10.02 Newcastle — Liverpool. No. 40 154 was following on a special, and was summoned with its train to push the express forward. It made a perfect start with its 19 coach load plus No. 46 055 on the gradient and headed off through Standedge tunnel towards Manchester. 31st July, 1976.
G.W. Morrison

Plate 231: Below No. 40 051 approaches Leeds (City) station on a breakdown train on 8th February, 1977.   G.W. Morrison

Plate 232: Left The end has come for these Class 40's Nos. 40 089/40 041/40 048 as they await breaking up at Eagle Bridge siding in Crewe Works on 19th February, 1978.

G.W. Morrison

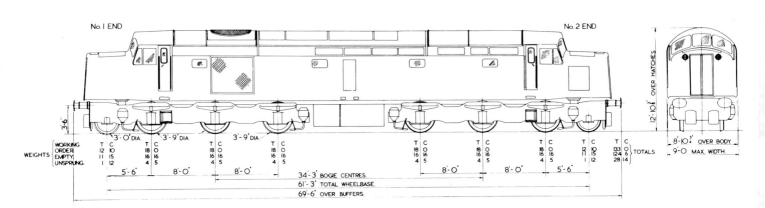

MAIN STATISTICS OF FORERUNNERS AND PRODUCTION FORTIES

	10000 10001	10201 10202	10203	FORTIES
Length over buffers	61 ft 2 ins	63 ft 9 ins	63 ft 9 ins	69 ft 6 ins
Overall width	9 ft 3 ins	9 ft 3 ins	9 ft 3 ins	9 ft 0 ins
Overall height	12 ft 11½ ins	13 ft 1 in	13 ft 1 in	12 ft 0 ins
Wheel diameter driving	3 ft 6 ins	3 ft 7 ins	3 ft 7 ins	3 ft 9 ins
Total wheelbase	51 ft 2 ins	55 ft 6 ins	55 ft 6 ins	61 ft 3 ins
Maximum speed	93 mph	90 mph	90 mph	90 mph
Maximum tractive effort	41,400 lb	48,000 lb	50,000 lb	52,000 lb
Continuous tractive effort	15,000 lb at 32 mph	21,700 lb at 24.5 mph	30,000 lb at 19.5 mph	30,900 lb at 18 mph
Axle layout	Co-Co	1 Co-Co 1	1 Co-Co 1	1 Co-Co 1
Engine model	16 SVT	16 SVT	16 SVT MK II	16 SVT MK II
Engine rating	1600 BHP at 750 rpm	1750 BHP at 850 rpm	2000 BHP at 850 rpm	2000 BHP at 850 rpm
Weight in working order	127 tons 13 cwt	135 tons 0 cwt	132 tons 16 cwt	124 tons 6 cwt to 134 tons 0 cwt
Fuel capacity	890 gallons	1150 gallons	1180 gallons	710 gallons